Before I was Born

Stacey Bellette

First published by Busybird Publishing 2024

Copyright © 2024 Stacey Bellette

ISBN:
Print: 978-1-923216-42-6

This work is copyright. Apart from any use permitted under the *Copyright Act 1968*, no part of this publication may be reproduced, stored in a retrieval system or transmitted in any form or by any means, electronic, mechanical, photocopying, recording or otherwise, without the prior written permission of Stacey Bellette.

The information in this book is based on the author's experiences and opinions. The author and publisher disclaim responsibility for any adverse consequences, which may result from use of the information contained herein. Permission to use any external content has been sought by the author. Any breaches will be rectified in further editions of the book.

Cover Image: Stacey Bellette

Cover design: Busybird Publishing

Layout and typesetting: Busybird Publishing

Busybird Publishing
2/118 Para Road
Montmorency, Victoria
Australia 3094
www.busybird.com.au

*This book is dedicated to my
family and my best friend Lisa.
And to all of my spirit family in heaven
who have helped me on my spiritual journey,
and for my readers, who breathe life into
these pages. I hope this book will give
everyone an understanding that we do
go on to live another special life.*

Contents

About the author   1

My early childhood   3

    Chapter 1   5

    Chapter 2 - Growing up   7

    Chapter 3   9

    Chapter 4   11

    Chapter 5 - Seeing spirit   13

    Chapter 6 - My daughter Bronwen   15

    Chapter 7   19 - All about spirits and how they affect you   19

Before I Was Born by Stacey Bellette   21

The afterlife for children   45

Afterlife communication, with children   47

About the author

My name is Stacey Kathleen Bellette, I was born on the 23rd of December, 1961. On my mum and dad's side there was four children and my parents. After my parents separated, I was living with my sisters and one brother. In time two more joined the family, Joanne and Janene. So all up six of us. Back in those days work was hard to find but Kevin, my stepdad, did everything he could for everyone to survive. I always liked old Kev, he never done wrong to any of us, and he worked all his life. I just can't remember how they met. But Mum and Kevey were happy. They were always there for us kids. I had a somewhat normal life as a child; went to school, didn't like it that much but oh well. Anyway, I knew I didn't belong at school. I belonged somewhere but not school, so I just did what kids did at home, watched Countdown, played dress ups, hung out with my dad before he died.

I love music and anything to do with art and I loved doing nursing for a short time and I had to leave because I had bad discs in my back. We lived on many farms most of my life, loved the country life. It was quiet and peaceful. When I think about my younger days when Dad kept telling me I was different I wish back then he would have told me that the gift was already there, I just didn't take any notice of it; it's been a long, hard road I've walked on but I'm still here and I'm now writing this book. And I do hope people enjoy reading it, as everything I wrote is very real. I am 62 years old now so I hope by speeding up my meditation I will touch base with more and more spirits.

My early childhood

Chapter 1

My childhood was pretty good, oh how I wish I could go back but, in saying that, I'm not so sure as every day was a lesson in life for me and many obstacles as well. School was a big one for me, I had to go to Sunday school and church with Mum many times, school was never meant for me as I wagged school so many times. I remember so many times walking down the long driveway of our house on the farm at Hodgson Vale to catch the school bus, many days, actually every day, I would zig-zag all the way down. If I got to the bus stop too early I'd jump in the long grass until the bus went past us, we all did it. So we snuck home only to find Mum in the house waiting for us to take us to school. Sometimes we got away with it, sometimes we didn't, this went on for many years and Mum was very angry with us but she got into a routine and took us to school. I could not outsmart mum in any way, it was impossible, so after a while we gave up and went to school.

I was getting older and I seemed to start liking school because I had made many friends in my school years, we went to so many different schools because Mum was always moving and couldn't settle in one town. I think that's why I didn't like it because I would make friends and then after a while we were moving again. I was pretty angry with Mum at the time and she explained why we were always moving: it was because of work, my mum had met another man after Dad was gone, his name was Kevin Zischke, I'm not sure how they met but he was pretty kind to us and worked very hard doing work on farms, in a piggery, driving tractors until all hours of the night. Kevin, aka Kevey, was okay and Mum found love for the second time in her life. Kevey took over from Dad and raised us the best way he could, I couldn't fault him for anything. I still missed my dad really badly, I never got over him, but life had to go on.

Life on a farm was pretty tough with many chores we had to do, and if we didn't do chores, we had to hear it from Mum. The strap would come out and there would be a scatter of kids running everywhere.

It was quite funny I'd have to say, Mum would tell me to hang up the washing only to find me outside hanging upside down on the clothesline while my sister Shirley would be spinning the clothesline around pretty fast until it broke. All I could do was look at my sister and run. It took Mum hours and hours to find us because the farm was massive, but we gave in and went back up to the house late in the afternoon for dinner but there was none for me and my sister, we were sent to our room.

Chapter 2
Growing up

Growing up was so horrible, I was in my teens, but some parts were pretty cool like when my cousin and his friends rode out to the farm on their motorbikes. We had so much fun getting doubled on the bikes around the farm, having a few drinks every weekend with my cousin Russell and my cousins mates, Dave and Tony.

It was a ritual for us and we were looking forward to every weekend. I was about fifteen at the time when Tony, my cousins friend, came out during the week in his car. Tony was twenty at the time, and he became really friendly with me. He was quite harmless and very friendly, I couldn't work out why Russell didn't come out, Tony said he was working. So, anyway, we were sitting in the lounge room one night watching a movie and Tony grabbed my hand, I quickly pulled my hand away and slapped him in the face. I didn't know what was going on until Mum came out and told me that Tony asked Mum if he could date me. So we did for a long time, nothing serious as I was pretty young and wasn't interested in a boyfriend. We kissed a couple of times and held hands, went for long drives. It was great, I'd look out of the window every night waiting for Tony's car to come down the long road leading to our house, every night for many weeks, and he stopped coming out. I was very upset at him and I thought he didn't like me anymore but that wasn't the case. My cousin came out on the weekend by himself and he told me that Tony got in trouble with the police. He was caught for drink driving and was locked up for a few months. And I forgot about him, life went on as usual, the fun stopped.

We went into town with Mum and Kevey and had dinner at the local pub one night. This man who was sitting in the bar drinking by himself walked past me to go to the toilet, he looked at me and smiled, he was very handsome, and I couldn't take my eyes off him. The next day me and Mum went to this old bakehouse to buy some bread, and he answered the door. I was shocked to see him, his name was Roger Hennessy. So, a long story short we met each other and started dating, I was sixteen at the time. Down the track I fell pregnant with my first born daughter, Bronwen. It was a massive shock for me as I was a kid having a kid, but I loved her so much when she was born. She was a screamer and a non-sleeper so no night life for me as I was too tired to do anything. Many years went by and I had my second daughter, Kathleen. She was a handful too but I loved her very much as well.

Their father went on and enjoyed his life drinking with his mates while I raised his two children. Life was bloody tough, the relationship was coming to an end after fifteen years together, I had to leave with my two girls because he became very violent towards us so I left. The hardest thing I had to do was walk away after fifteen years, if I didn't things would have got worse and I couldn't have my daughters living in that environment. A little while after the separation Roger passed away at the age of forty from a massive heart attack.

Chapter 3

It wasn't hard bringing up my girls on my own as Roger never helped me anyway. They were growing up fast, I put them through school and did my best for them, I wish I could have given them a better life financially, but I couldn't. So I made do with what we had, they have their own lives to live now and families of their own. Also, my beautiful grandchildren, Toa, Tane, Dillon, Samanatha, Rebecca, and the new addition from my son Justin, little Noah. How blessed am I to have my family? I wouldn't change it for anything in the world. After Roger passed away, I was in another relationship that only lasted for six years, but the best thing from that one was my boy, Justin. I love him very much, he's such a kind and caring person towards everyone, as my daughters are too. After that relationship failed, I gave up and I thought, "Well, what now, what do I do with my life?"

I did nursing for a while, which I loved very much. I always wanted to help other people all my life but never new how. I did lots of stuff throughout my life but I wasn't satisfied with my life, I knew there was something I had to do and it took many hard lessons in life to get the right answer, and this is who I am and who I want to be up until it's my turn to cross over.

I'm a very honest person and I still have lots to learn about my gift. I am not fake and I'd never read any person unless I can validate the reading to that client. It doesn't happen overnight and being a medium, I would have to say, is the hardest job in the world. We are always learning different things every day. It never stops, it's a lifelong commitment and it's a gift you take with you when you die. So, I'm thinking this gift is earned by life's lessons, you have to survive the worst of the worst and I think back to the day I had my heart attack. I wasn't scared, it really didn't bother me at all and when I saw my father standing beside me telling me I would be okay, I knew then I wasn't going anywhere anytime soon. I'm here for a reason and that reason is to help those who have lost loved ones and not convince, but validate, to them that nobody else would know what their loved one has said .

Chapter 4

My father travelled all over the place to do his rides, to places I don't even know. What a wonderful life that would have been for him, as that was his job, like everybody else has jobs. There's no way you could ever get Dad off a horse. Ever since I found out that dad took his life I've been so angry for over thirty long years but then I sat down and thought about it. He wasn't in good health and he was one of those people that didn't believe in going to the doctor when he was sick. He was a very stubborn person, always thought he could fix himself by having a drink, but strong liquor ate away his insides, and not only he couldn't ride anymore or have his family back, he gassed himself in his unit with his gas stove.

I forgave him for what he did and, ever since I did that, Dad showed up more and talked to me all the time. He always says to me when I'm not recording, "You're Daddy's little girl." He would pop in every now and then and I could hear him saying to me, "How are your kids?" I have several recordings of Dad talking and all I can do is cry and smile at the same time. He's with Mum now. They still argue a bit like they did when they were alive and Mum even gets jealous in spirit like she did when they were alive.

If it wasn't for my dad I wouldn't be the person I am today. He always told me to respect people and help out in any way I can. That is part of the gift: the more you put into it, the more you get back. If only I could go back in time to when I was sixteen, I would have put more effort into finding Dad and bringing him home with me so I could look after him for the rest of my life. It hurts very much having to go back to the past and talk about Dad, but I have to. It's, in a way, a healing process for me, and I know Dad will be the first one there to collect me when its my turn to go, and I'd have to say I'm looking forward to seeing all my spirit people again.

Chapter 5
Seeing spirit

Seeing spirits for the very first time was very overwhelming, I never believed in this sort of stuff ever. Believe it or not, I was the biggest sceptic alive. I thought that this sort of stuff was only seen on television and not in real life, so when it came out stronger and stronger I didn't know what to do and who to tell. My family didn't believe me and I went to great lengths to prove that what I was seeing and hearing was real. I even went as far as going to the local newspaper with proof of what I had. The editor told me that they would run it through their equipment and if it wasn't real it wouldn't be published, so the next day it was in the paper. And after all that, still, no one believed me. This is something you cannot make up, this was the real deal. Sceptics hammered me into the ground and it was quite heartbreaking for no one to believe me. I wouldn't lie or go through all this trouble to prove to people that there is life after life. I'm not sure if people believe me today but, you know what? I really don't care because I know it's real and I am not and never will be afraid of death.

A spirit once told me that heaven was beautiful, it's like the galaxy; different levels and dimensions that we travel through. My sister Shirley also came to me and told me that she can't talk to me much because she was having a life review. I saw her walk into a tall building, like a tower of some sort, there were long white curtains and a white chair sitting in the middle of the floor. She sat down on it and waved goodbye to me with a beautiful smile and then she was gone.

I have seen so many spirits I've lost count. When I was living beside my neighbour, Lisa, I looked at her face and, in seconds, this other face of an elderly lady appeared in Lisa's face. All I could do was stare and then proceeded to tell her what I saw; it was an older version of my neighbour.

This face had red lipstick on, blue eye shadow on and was dressed up like she was going to some event. Lisa then told me it sounded like her grandmother, she then pulled her photo album out and found a picture of her, and oh gosh I was just shocked. There is also an old lady called Dorothy still living in Lisa's unit, I have caught her on camera a couple of times. She's harmless, very kind, but doesn't like getting her picture taken. She loves her unit and just sits in the lounge minding her own business. She would often let herself be known to me and when she was around. God bless her. I could sit here and write about so many spirits but there is just too much to talk about.

You're probably wondering what a spirit is. Well, in my opinion, a spirit is energy. It takes a lot of energy to even get a few words out and an enormous amount of energy to show themselves. They can also interfere with mobiles, televisions, radios etc. They can hide things sometimes for a few days, weeks or months, and, sometimes, you might even get the item back that is missing or it could turn up in a different place altogether. They can mimic your voice, tell you all these wonderful things and trick you as well. But it took me a while to work it out so I just respond to my family in spirit for now and, yes, I get thousands of random spirits all the time. It takes a while to get used to them but I have no choice. Sometimes I just shut down and tell them to all go away and I will call on them when needed. One thing I had to learn was meditation, that's the hard part. I find that waves are the best way to connect with a spirit, and a lot of deep breathing. Once I'm in a routine it gets a bit better.

Chapter 6

My daughter Bronwen

My first born was Bronwen. She was born on the 20th of November, 1978. She was a very cranky baby. She didn't believe in sleeping so she gave me a run for my money, what a little screamer she was. She was a good weight and very healthy, she was hardly ever sick as a child. Her father was a different story, I found out that he had a heart attack at the age of 18 and never told me for many years. As time passed, so did he, at the age of 40, from a massive heart attack.

In years to follow many more family members died from the same thing. Unfortunately, it was hereditary and, around about 2021, Bronwen was having slight chest pain but put it down to something she might have eaten. So, she ignored it and went back to doing the things she had to do like being a cleaner for many years. At the end of October she seemed to be getting worse and lost so much weight. She rang me up one day in a panic and told me she couldn't breathe properly, so I quickly made an appointment for her to see the doctor. And, in saying that, I'm glad I did because we found out she had heart failure. It was the most shocking thing I've heard the doctor say, I just went numb and Bronwen broke down in the surgery.

I knew for a long time she wasn't well and I was always on her back to go to the doctor for a complete checkup but she would never listen to me. I rang my grandson on the 1st of November, my son's birthday. I had a horrible feeling in my gut that this was going get bad so I told my grandson to take her up to the hospital ASAP. No time wasted, I went up half an hour after that, but she looked okay so I wasn't concerned at that stage. At about 3.00 am in the morning my youngest daughter, Kathleen, was knocking on the door of my van. She came in with Bronwen's son,

Dillon, on the phone. Bronwen was on the end of it also. I didn't know what the hell was going on and then Dillon told me that at about 2.30 in the morning they were called up to the hospital because Bronwen's heart had stopped several times, and she was going to be airlifted to the Prince Alfred Hospital in Brisbane for further treatment. My daughter came on the phone and told me not to worry and that she would be okay. By then, tears started pouring out and I couldn't stop. All my life bad stuff was just continuous. I felt like I was being punished for some reason but didn't know why.

After a few days, Bronwen was getting worse and worse to the point where they had to transfer her to the Prince Charles Hospital because they had the equipment there to treat her. Bronwen was placed in an induced coma because her heart couldn't take anymore shocks from the paddles on her chest. There was so much damage to her heart and so many arteries that had to be burned off, plus a huge blood clot in her heart to make things worse. When I first went down to see her it looked like she was in a serious road accident, life support connected, wires running inside of her legs and outside all the way up to her neck. A temporary pacemaker was inserted into her neck and god knows what else. It was something no parent should see, so we suffered the trauma right alongside Bronwen. The doctors made several video calls to discuss treatment and the survival rate was a 50/50 chance, one doctor even wanted us to switch the life support machine off and that's when all hell broke loose.

We were called into the office and told by this lady doctor that obviously didn't know how to do her job that we were prolonging my daughters passing. I stood up, I looked at her, I looked at the door, and walked out because, if I didn't, things would have gotten really bad for the doctor. How dare anyone saying that to a mother whose child/daughter was very unwell? I walked out of the hospital to cool off and then my youngest daughter dealt with the doctor. The many battles and arguments we had with everyone down there shouldn't have happened, so my other daughter made it quite clear that they had to find another way to save her, and many operations later the surgeons did just that. They saved my daughter and she has many stents and a pacemaker and is doing great. I remember asking Dad to be with her and not let her die, and after several weeks in hospital Bronwen started telling us how she saw five spirits standing around her bed telling her that it wasn't her time to go. Yes, I believe in miracles, and one happened with my daughter. She is alive and doing great.

Spiritual Quotes

"Just as a candle cannot burn without fire, man cannot live without a spiritual life."

– Buddha

"Awakening is not changing who you are, but discarding who you are not."

– Deepak Chopra

"The privilege of a lifetime is to become who you really are."

– Carl Jung

"You have to grow from the inside out. No one can teach you; no one can make you spiritual. There is no other teacher but your own soul."

– Swami Vivekananda

"If you do a good job for others, you heal yourself at the same time, because a dose of joy is a spiritual cure. It transcends all barriers."

– Ed Sullivan

"You are never alone. You are eternally connected with everyone."

– Amit Ray

"We are not human beings having a human experience. We are spiritual beings having a human experience."

– Pierre Teilhard de Chardin

Chapter 7
All about spirits and how they affect you

Before I found out who I was I thought I was just an average person, I never in my wildest dreams thought that spirit would choose me to have this very special gift. The downside is they never go away. They're with me 24/7. Once you have contact with spirit it's just a roller coaster ride that never stops and I'm not exaggerating. They talk more than me, they play tricks on you, there's so many things they can do. The worst part is, because spirit is energy there's always lots of headaches, they don't stop, it's quite annoying really. When I sense a spirit around, I can usually pick up their emotions, like, if they were sad, I will be too and so on. That is called empathy, another thing that comes with this wonderful gift, and please, please don't call spirit a ghost. If you ask me what a ghost is I'll just look at you. If you ask me what a spirit is then I can answer the question.

Ghosts are so overrated, it's a word that's used in movies, and all these horror movies are just made up, they give spirits a bad name. Real spirits don't go around scaring people, they come with much love and messages. Yes, they can mimic people and tell you all sorts of wonderful things that mightn't be true, so, if you have an encounter with one and this spirit is not related to you then you have a trickster playing games with you. It's happened to me a million times. Spirits do not just come out at night time as a lot of people think. They come out during the day as I've seen many times myself. Yes, they can be in the toilet with you, in the shower, well, not under water but I've seen them through the shower curtain. It really doesn't bother me anymore because I'm used to it. Now I just say to them "Thanks for the visit and come back anytime you want," but sometimes you have to be polite and tell them to leave. But one thing that is very important to me is respect towards the spirit. It's a massive, big must, and always say please and thank you. They can hear you and see every little thing you do so never speak bad of the dead.

The other thing I like doing is recording them on my laptop. You can actually record them on anything, like your phone, voice recorder, iPod ... just about anything. I love doing this so people can actually hear what I hear, and I usually tell people if they can't hear it to use earphones or headphones. You would be surprised at what you will hear. Nearly everybody has an ability, you just have to be more open to it and you have to learn to listen. But I can't stress enough: meditation is the key. It's very hard at first and you're better off doing it in a quiet place where you won't be disturbed. Practice makes perfect, they say. And it's true.

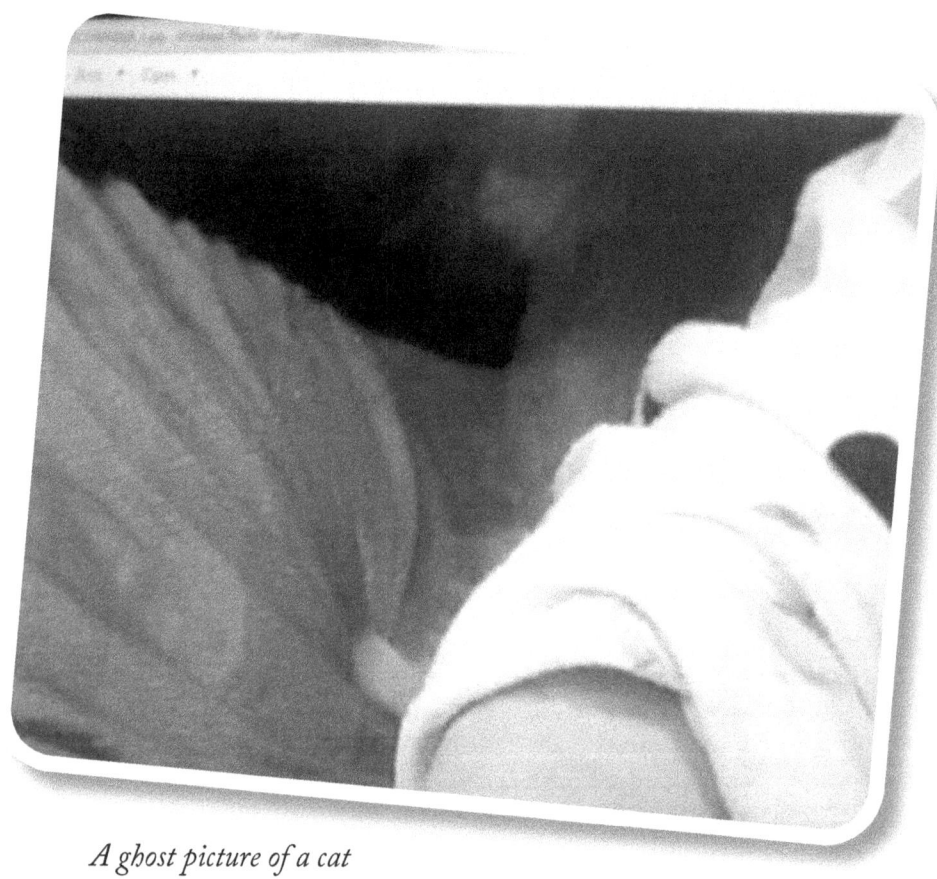

A ghost picture of a cat

Before I Was Born by Stacey Bellette

My father's anniversary of his passing is on the 4th of September. That day I was standing in my caravan at 11.30 am. I was sipping on my cup of tea when I felt a presence. I looked out of my van window and saw a full, solid apparition of my father walking down the ramp which leads into the house. He continued to walk towards my van, but I wasn't shocked as I've seen him many times before. He had his favorite flannelette shirt on that he would wear after he had finished riding and his old, blue pair of jeans. And I knew it was Dad because of his strawberry colored hair; red/blonde. 9.30 pm that same night, I was very unsettled, so I got up and made a cup of tea, I was sitting down just trying to relax and a voice, as clear as crystal, told me "I love you," and I replied. And then it dawned on me that it was Dad because he then said, "You're Daddy's little girl." He always told me that in life and in spirit. Dad took his own life on the 4th of September, 1977 and, without a miss, he's always there.

But Dad doesn't need an occasion to be around me, he's with me all the time, wherever I go he's looking out for me. I lived in many houses, always moving from house to house. For many years, I lived in a high-set rental for six years, after my sister passed that's when everything started again but it was getting less annoying. I got out of bed to get a bottle of water and I stopped myself in the doorway because I saw this black figure floating towards me, it was the size of a child. I'm like, "Nope" and jumped in bed and went straight under the blankets and that's where I stayed until morning.

> My daughter Bronwen, aged 44, it would have been a couple of years back, and I immediately knew when I went over for a visit one day, that Bronwen was down in the dumps. I sat down with her for a chat she looked at me and pulled her shirt up and showed me her ribs. I was mortified as to what I saw, I could count every rib in her body. She burst into tears, but

getting Bronwen to a doctor was very hard because she was so stubborn, I guess she gets that from me. As time went on we were busy with our lives but still caught up on social media like Facebook. On the 1st of November, 2023, Bronwen became ill. She rang me up very distraught and crying, and I quickly made an appointment for her to see my doctor. She wanted to go this time because she knew she was very sick. Blood tests and chest x-rays proved that Bronwen was facing a battle. She became worse so Dillon, her son, took her to the hospital under strict instructions from myself; I told him to get her up there ASAP and I would be up there soon. I was getting ready to go to the hospital, and I was there nearly all day. I got her lunch, and she was happy because she told me she was in a safe place now. At 2.30 pm my other daughter arrived, then at my van at about 3.30 pm my grandson Dillon was on the phone, telling me Bronwen had to be shocked with paddles three times. I was beyond shocked, I thought that she might have had a chest infection but it was much more than that. She was airlifted to the Prince Alfred Hospital straight away.

I couldn't go back to sleep because I was so upset and started keeping myself busy by cleaning up, and then it happened again. Dad walked past my van as though he was heading in the direction of Brisbane. I knew where he was going, I told him to look after my daughter for me; my daughter was in a critical condition and hooked up to life support. This was the most horrible thing in my life. I had to watch, and there was nothing I could do.

For eight days straight all I could do was cry, and cry, and cry. I couldn't eat or sleep and I couldn't get my daughters face out of my head. No parent should have to go through that. My Aunty Marge had twelve children and buried four of them, I really don't know how she survived, and now I'm facing the same battle with my daughter, Bronwen. I got back from the hospital pretty late, and tried to have some dinner but I just couldn't eat anything. I called on my father to stay beside Bronwen and not to let her die. She was getting ready for her operation that day I was there, I cried all over her and begged her not to leave me. Over and over and over, I just repeated myself, and then this strange feeling came over me, it was a calming feeling. I had a feeling she was going to be okay.

The next morning I rang the hospital and the surgeon told me that she was going to be okay. She had a very rough night after surgery but she was stable and doing okay. After the operation, she had to have her heart shocked a few times to get the rhythm of her heart beating properly. She is responding well to all medication and she even had some machines removed but still needs life support. My daughter is not out of the woods yet, she has a very long road to recovery. My son, Justin, told me the next morning that Bronwen's voice was heard at about 11.30 pm when my son couldn't sleep. He heard her say loud and clear to tell Mum that she would be okay. He couldn't believe what he was hearing and my son doesn't lie about serious things like that. So, in saying that, I feel that Bronwen must have astral travelled, and it's funny, because she told me the same thing; that she would be okay. Touch wood everything is going well so far and I hope and pray my miracle girl survives this horrible thing she is facing. My father is constantly around me talking to me, reassuring me that my daughter is going to be okay.

With more surgery coming up to remove a temporary pacemaker from her neck and into her chest, this also can be quiet serious as she is so very weak. Every time an operation is mentioned, my heart stops. My daughter will never be the same daughter I had before, but she's so strong and trying her hardest to fight for life, and I know that while my father is with her he won't let her go.

Delirium has set in now and it's been five days. We were told it could last as long as two weeks or more, and what breaks my heart is seeing my child trying to talk and trying to pull herself out of bed. It just kills me. Sometimes she knows who we are and then she doesn't; it's on and off all the time. The hardest part is when we think everything is going okay there's always a setback. If my heart wasn't sick also, and she needed a transplant, I would have stepped up and demanded the surgeons to give her mine, but we are all praying it doesn't get to that stage. So it's baby steps one day at a time, all we can do now is just hope she fully recovers. She's definitely my miracle baby. I will not give up on my daughter. Never in a million years. The loss of a child before a parent should never happen. I always asked my aunty how she coped. She had twelve children and buried four, and now I know how she felt because I'm going through the same thing, but I'm not giving up on her, not ever. It just isn't her time to go yet and I'll make sure of that.

All my life my family has been through hell and back. Life has thrown some very hard balls at us, but we are still standing and will continue to keep standing beside our loved ones because that's what family does. It doesn't matter how old they are, at the end of the day they're still my children. You never stop being a parent, it is a life long contract.

Spirit keep guiding me 24/7, and I'm so glad to have this gift because I knew there was something wrong with my daughter two years ago. I always nagged her to go for a checkup, but, being the stubborn person she is, she always came up with an excuse. But then, as time went on she rang me straight away. I got her up to my doctor and had several tests done and found out the worst news I've ever heard. Wasting no time, I knew she had to go into hospital, she said to me, "Mum, I'm happy now," and I feel safe that someone is going to help her. At 2.30pm she was asleep and was woken up by doctors putting paddles on her chest to bring her back. I lost count after about 30 times, and that's when my nightmare started.

She can't walk yet, can't eat, slowly talking a bit but it's better than nothing. I could have buried my daughter but she fought and is still trying. Bronwen went into hospital on the 1st of November, my sons birthday, so it's pretty easy to know how long she's been in hospital for, and now she's getting bedsores. She's in so much pain and no matter what we do, or the doctors do, nothing seems to help, but I'm so grateful she is still with us. At about 1.50 pm on Thursday the 23rd of November, 2023 I called the Prince Charles Hospital about my daughter, not expecting what I was going to hear, but the news was awesome. Bronwen was out of bed and sitting in a chair. The nurse put the phone on loudspeaker for us so I could talk to her but, because of all the tubes that were down her throat, she could only whisper, but I heard most of what she said, and she kept telling me that she loved me. I reassured her that she was safe and that not only myself but the rest of the family loved her, too, and she sounded so happy. After the call I just dropped to my knees and cried like a baby knowing my girl was on the mend. But the worst part of everything that's happened to her: anything could go wrong. Fingers crossed nothing will, I just want my girl back home.

Miracles are real. Just like spirit, they stand beside a loved one and put all the energy into that person to heal them, and I would swear on the Bible that it was my father looking over her. He loved his children and grandkids, that's just the sort of dad he was. So, in saying that, angels are real. I truly believe angels are our loved ones that have crossed over. Many hundreds of recordings later, and still climbing, is proof that we don't really die, we absolutely do come back. I can't express it enough and I hope that when someone reads my book that they too can have some peace of mind knowing that their loved ones walk beside them every day. The human body is like a shell of an old car, but the soul and spirit live on forever in another dimension in the galaxy.

I always thought, "Why me? Why did they have to choose me to have this gift?" But then I sat down and accepted it, and as soon as you accept it that's when my gift really kicked in. I was seeing full apparitions in what was broad daylight. Spirit playing games with me when I went shopping by picking up my hair and making it stand up in the air, turning lights on and off in the supermarket and laughing at me. Heaps of stuff. It was like something out of a movie. But now I have to say that I love my gift and I'm so glad I have it, otherwise my daughter wouldn't be alive today. So, to everyone out there please believe me when I say this: we don't really die.

Going back to my unit in Sunning Street, Toowoomba, I have to say that I met, out of seven other tenants, one lady in particular, her name is Lisa Baker, we connected straight away. We had so much in common. It was weird, it was like I was her and she was me. She helped me settle in and spoke to me in a very nice manner. Her parents, John and Carmel, raised a beautiful person. I was only in my unit for six months before it was sold on me. I was so heartbroken, but the amount of fun and the things we did in such a short time were the best days of my life. To this day we are still mates and catch up when we can. She's smart, well educated, funny, and always makes me laugh when I'm feeling down. Lisa always gives me the right advice when it's needed. Lisa herself is also gifted in many ways and I've told her so, but she too has lived a traumatic life and just has trouble accepting things just as I did. Lisa is my best friend forever, you don't need 100 friends, or 20 friends, or even 2 friends. You only need one honest, good friend and that's all I need in my life.

So many spirits appeared inside of Lisa's unit. There was an old lady called Dorothy who sadly passed away in the unit. To this day, Dorothy is still there and showed herself to me many times, and I have captured a couple of pictures of her. Dorothy was in her late 80s when she crossed over to the spirit world.

When Lisa's grandmother appeared in Lisa's face, I couldn't work out why she was wearing lipstick because Lisa doesn't wear lipstick and makeup. I then knew it was not her, but someone who would have been related to her. Lisa told me her grandmother wore red lipstick to her wedding, so when Lisa showed me a photo I nearly died because I saw the face of her grandmother in Lisa's face. It was a message for Lisa to let her know she's watching over her.

Pretty much just about everyone is gifted in many ways, you just have to be more open to it. It definitely isn't easy being a medium/clairvoyant, because there is a lot involved like accepting it first, and learning about the new you. Meditating is the biggest lesson of all time, and without that it's nearly impossible to connect with spirit. You have to learn how to interpret messages from spirit to the grieving, and I would never read anyone if I couldn't validate a message to a person that only that person knew. I've done a couple readings that I actually saw after I meditated. So, yes, it's a very hard job being who we are, it's no bed of roses that's for sure. I am by no means looking to be famous in any way, I just want to tell the world what I know. I have seen some most beautiful moments in my life with spirit and, believe me, they can also tell wonderful stories too. They can interfere with televisions, radios, mobile phones, electricity, move small objects etc. Because they are energy, they can come and go whenever they want. They're not in pain or sick anymore, it's just the physical body we miss, but as soon as they cross over they are by your side straight away. I have witnessed these events.

As I'm sitting here writing this they are annoying the heck out of me by tugging on my hair. They love that one. The only downfall about being a medium is spirit drains you like a battery. So we also need to shut down and take a break. This path was given to us for a reason, we must have the utmost respect for spirit and always thank them for there help. Life's biggest lessons are very painful, like childhood traumas after I found out my dad took his own life, and then in 2000 my sister did the same thing. I would have to say I've suffered traumas my whole life right into my adult life, with very bad relationships and so on. Many times, I wanted to leave this Earth just to have some peace but the only thing that kept me here was my children. If I never had them, to be honest, I wouldn't be here. Even after my heart attack in 2019 I was so angry that I survived. I thought I was being tortured by something. I just wanted to be with my heavenly family, but I wasn't even allowed to do that.

After the heart attack my appendix burst. I was doubled over in pain, something I can't stand is pain. So I went to the hospital and had many tests done but they couldn't find anything, so, I was sent home, only to get worse by the second. My daughter made me make an appointment to see my doctor. It took one blood test to find out that my appendix had burst. I just got through the door when my doctor rang me and told me to get up to the hospital ASAP, and I was admitted into hospital that same day. As bad as I was it still took the doctors three days to operate. Then the next day I was showered and prepped for the operation but, because of the heart attack, they had to check my blood type before they could operate in case I started bleeding. So, that took nearly two hours in the hallway.

The operation was done and I was back in the ward. I was so sore I couldn't even walk, I must have been in hospital for eight days, but in that time frame so many spirits were watching over me. Even random ones, and, yes, my dad was with me every step of the way. He always reassured me that I'd be okay but, to be honest, I didn't care anymore if I lived or died because I'm not afraid of death. Because of what I know, I'm more afraid of life, to be honest Because, being human, we experience everything and so much pain throughout our life. I actually look forward to the day I cross over because I know my dad will be the first one there to collect me. Every family member in my family has experienced the presence of spirit, my daughter Kathleen, Bronwen, Justin, Sam, Dillon, Bronwen's partner Les. The list is endless.

So, back in hospital trying to recover. I managed to drag myself out of bed. Doubled over in pain, I made it to the toilet when all of a sudden I heard a man's voice as clear as day, like he was in the bathroom with me. He said, "Hello Stacey, my name is John, why are you in hospital?" I'm like, really? Geez, give me a break. So, back to bed I went. At about 3.00 am in the morning I was woken up by this strange nurse. I was fully having a good chat to her, I looked at her and asked why was she wearing an army costume. When I questioned her she changed the subject very quickly, and I noticed on her left arm when she was checking my board, that she had a red cross band on her arm. I said to her, "Who are you?" She just told me to rest up and that I'd be okay. She turned to walk away but went straight through the curtain. As sore as I was, I flew out of bed and never saw her walking down the hallway. The next day I asked the nurses about her and they must have thought I was crazy, so I searched her online and found her. She did work at the base before I was even born. I wasn't shocked at all it was her nursing spirit checking up on me. Such a beautiful thing that happened that night, I will never forget anything that I've experienced.

Night four and two girls were screaming at three in the morning. I was awake so I know what I heard, again I scrambled out of bed and ran into the hallway, but there was no one there. One nurse came out of the nurses' station and asked me why was I out of bed. I told her about the two girls screaming in the hallway in pain, she then said, "There's no one here." She went back to the nurses' station, I turned around and saw this pretty young lady about 22 years of age, it looked like she had been in a car accident. She looked at me smiling and I asked her if she was okay, but no reply. I followed her into the ward, I wasn't far behind her, I offered my help but when I went into the bathroom to assist her, she vanished. I asked a patient if they saw a young lady walking into the ward and one lady said, "No." So I went back to my room, got in bed and fell asleep. The rest of my stay at hospital was pretty quiet after that. At least they were giving me a break. It's hard to live a normal life when millions of spirit go wherever I go. This is a 24/7 thing. Sometimes when people look at me I get so paranoid that some of them can see spirit as well, so I usually power walk in the supermarkets just to get out.

A mirror is like taboo to me, I can't look into a mirror for long periods of time as a mirror is a portal for spirit. Many things showed up in mirrors like an actual outline of a head with every section of the head explained. That was very overwhelming to say the least. Love hearts were appearing, spirits were showing themselves to me and so much more, it's absolutely fascinating to witness these things that I see. My dad always told me I was different, but had no idea I was going to be this person who could communicate with spirit. It took me many years to accept my gift, and it's definitely something you can't just blurt out in a normal conversation so, yes, it's been a tough life with this gift. But I've learnt so much about so many things and also myself, but now I wouldn't change anything in the world. Normal life would be so boring.

But please know that your loved ones are very much still with you, I cannot express it enough. They are with you, they show you signs every day, they are not in any pain at all, they come to you in dreams. So pay attention to that one because dreams are not always dreams. Their physical body might be gone and we all miss that so much, but their soul and spirit live on forever. Just think of it in a different way that they didn't die, they went home. Yes, we love our loved ones, and we don't want to see them go but, unfortunately, death is a part of life. We all have to go at some stage in our life, but always remember that they lived and loved and they still do. Remember all the memories and the good times you had with your people. Talk to them because, yes, they're still here, they can see you and touch you and they try so hard to get a message through to you. Just be more open to it all.

Back to my beautiful daughter, Bronwen. Bronwen was born on the 20th of November, 1978. I was sixteen when I gave birth to her. Wow, was she a handful. She certainly gave me a run for my money … sleep … what was that? A screamer every day and night, she hardly ever slept. I could not calm her down, she was a newborn going on 18. She continued to grow up very stubborn and spoke her mind when she had to, and fought like a man. I had to check a few times to see if she was a girl or a boy. But, in saying that, I was the same.

Two years before her 45th birthday she wasn't well at all, I knew she wasn't, I nagged her so many times to have a good check up but, nope, she wouldn't. She kept working as a cleaner at several places in Toowoomba up until the 1st of November. She became really sick to the point where she had no choice but to go to the doctor, so I made an appointment for her to see my doctor. A couple days later we got the results back and it wasn't good news.

The nightmare started. She was told she had a bad heart, I tried to take her to the hospital that day, but, being as stubborn as she is, would not go. I rang my sister Jo up and told her. My sister called Bronwen and had a really good talk to her, so Bronwen agreed to go to the base hospital. She was happy, she told me that she felt safe now because someone was going to help her as she couldn't breath properly. I brought Bronny some lunch because she was so thin; a sausage roll, orange juice and some fruit salad. She ate the lot and I sat there until she did. She became sad, so I tried to cheer her up by putting gloves on my hands and feet and started waving to anyone that walked past. It worked because she laughed so hard, and so did the nursing staff.

At 2.30 in the morning Bronwen was in bed sleeping and she was woken up by the nurses and paddles on her chest. She didn't know what the heck was going on, the poor girl. I got a wake up call from my other daughter, Kathleen, banging on my caravan door. She came in and just told me what had happened to Bronny. I was in shock, so her son Dillon was on the phone. I spoke to Bronwen for a short while, she said, "Mum, I'll be okay." Tears were pouring down so fast I just couldn't stop. I was numb. And then she was flown to the Prince Alfred Hospital in Brisbane. She spent a few days there but they couldn't work out what was wrong with her, so then she was moved to the Prince Charles Hospital in Brisbane. Several tests were done and it wasn't good at all. She had so much damage to her heart that even the surgeons didn't think she was going to make it. There were so many arguments every day about saving my daughters life. Finally, we got a surgeon who wanted to operate to give her a chance of survival. It was very risky but we were running out of time and I wasn't ready to let my girl go. All up, she had three operations. After about nine hours work on her, that was it for me, I called on my dad to go and protect Bronwen. I actually saw him walk past my van as though he was heading in the direction of Brisbane. A few days later we were getting updates about Bronwen. She was starting to pick up, and each day she was getting better. Today, on the 24th of November, 2023, I spoke to Bronwen on the phone for about 25 minutes and that, I have to say, is my miracle child. She has a long way to go yet but it's baby steps for her, one day at a time and more surgery down the track. But I'm so grateful she is alive.

Your whole life can change in seconds. Please don't play with your health because we only have one life and that can be taken away at any time. My daughter was so strong as a baby, a child. And, as an adult, she survived the biggest trauma in her life, and, as a mother I swear I'll look after her until my dying days.

I myself had a heart attack in 2019, so I cant even imagine how Bronwen is feeling right now. She needs a lot of care and counselling but I will stand beside my girl every step of the way. I'm trying to find another word higher than a miracle and when I do, that will be my girl Bronwen. She's young, beautiful, kind and funny and very strong. She told me on the phone that she wasn't that strong anymore until I corrected her. She's even stronger now because she escaped death. For someone to come back from all the medical problems she had, and still has, that in itself is stronger than strong. She knew it wasn't her time to go and I truly believe she was being watched over by many of those that loved her in spirit.

I remember a dream of hundreds I had about my beloved sister after she passed. She came to me straight away, as spirits can do that, she told me that she can't talk much because she was in the middle of a life review. So many things spirit attend to after they cross over. I myself have never seen heaven and won't know myself until it's my time, but I honestly believe that heaven is a dimension in the galaxy. There are different levels for spirit. If I'm correct I'm sure there's about 10 all up. As I said in my book, I saw stars and the galaxy when I was watching down on my parents getting married. We are all put on this Earth for a reason. I knew I was here for some reason but just couldn't work it out, but now I know why I'm here and that's to help as many people as I can. Intuition is a very big part of being a medium, "We shall allow our intuition to guide us," mine never lets me down, ever. And, again, meditation is a must. I usually listen to theta beats, the main one to contact spirit, but lots and lots of this meditation is very important to receive good results. It's not just a big job, it's a huge responsibility as well.

Like I said, I wouldn't read anyone if I didn't have their people come in, and, sometimes, they don't want to talk. I asked the spirit of an old man one night to come in and talk to me. He was very blunt and replied a "No" answer to me, so you can't always get what you want. Some spirits can come in and tell you all these wonderful stories that probably aren't true. They are very cunning and stubborn, as I too have had this experience.

I think the best part of my gift is seeing full, solid apparitions. Like having lunch with my family in a pub in Laidley, Queensland. I'm sitting near two glass doors with a bell above the door. I never heard the bell, nor did the doors open, but when I looked to the left of me I saw an old man slowly walking past me. He was a patient at the nursing home where my mum was staying at. I said, "Oh, sorry," and moved my chair out of the way, but he vanished just as he got past me. I turned to look at my sister's partner, who gave me a strange look and called out to my sister who was at the bar getting some soft drinks, "Janene! Your sister is talking to ghosts again." I couldn't help but laugh. But, yes, it was the old man's spirit looking for my mother as he liked Mum very much. He had passed away on the day we were having lunch. Not every medium is perfect, even the best of the best get things wrong. It's about getting a name, or a letter, or they can say many things that can be identified by the person getting a reading. There's just so much to this and, for the medium, it's a very tough position to have. But, all in all, I love my gift and I wouldn't swap it for anything in the world, not that I can. But you're born with it and you die with it.

Life is very unpredictable; fine one day, the next clinging to life. But when my daughter was given back to us, every day it's a massive effort for my girl to battle life but I know how strong she is. Fighting a chest infection and a very badly infected bedsore are only a couple of her problems. I know she won't be home for Christmas, but we will all be there at the hospital for her with lots of presents and lots of love. I love you, Bronwen, to the moon and back. They say only the good die young, well, not this girl. No way is my girl going to heaven yet because she's needed here with her family. On the 28th of November, 2023 I talked to my daughter on the phone. She is slowly getting her voice back, we had the best talk ever. She told me that there were five spirits standing near her bed and that an elderly man in his 90s spoke to her. He then told her that it wasn't her time yet. Bronwen's words were, "He said 'It's not your time yet, Missy,'" and I remember her grandfather, Andrew Hennessy, used to call her that as a child. She then went on to tell me that she heard cracking sounds and the lights in the hospital began to flicker.

Before all this happened to Bronwen she used to tell me about a lot of spirits visiting her at home, and I know for a fact that all the females on my side are gifted. It goes way back to our ancestors, all the females were gifted. I still to this day don't understand why I was chosen to be one of these gifted people. There is sixty-one years of stories to talk about so this is my life now. I wouldn't do anything else but talk to my spirit people. I used to be so scared of death when I was a child but, now that I know what I know, I'm not frightened of death at all. It's life that scares the hell out of me, as we have to deal with problems in this world: war, disasters, and sickness, and everything else. Life is just a big test, like going to school, and when we pass over we are at peace, and we sure do come back. The hardest part about this gift is learning a whole new life. Being a medium is hard and, again, it's another learning curve. So many lessons to learn. Hours and hours of recording spirit talking so I could prove to the world we do come back and this, I swear, is the truth. My journey with the spirit world will still go on even after I'm gone. Hey, at least we can go anywhere in the world and not have to worry about paying for anything, which is a bonus.

A few years back I was invited to Sydney to do a conference with Mr Robb Tilley, a paranormal investigator, from the Australian Institute of Parapsychological Research. I would have loved to have gone over to meet Mr Tilley, but I am afraid of heights and aeroplanes so I didn't make it. One day I hope to go but travel some other way. Mr Tilley was also very gifted, so there's millions of us out there, you just have to be careful who you get a reading from.

So, back to my daughter. Every day is a struggle for her, she can't walk properly yet but she's trying. Her whole life was turned upside down, as mine was from my heart attack and my sister's heart attack. But, unfortunately, it's hereditary so no one is safe. I still have four more blockages in my heart that are controlled by medication. But I'm not scared because if something happens again and I don't make it I have no regrets. This is life, we can only do the best we can. My poor, beautiful daughter, how are we going to ever come to terms with what happened to you? Life isn't fair. Life is very cruel. You have a very long way to go, a very long road to recovery, but your whole family is standing beside you forever. You will never be alone. It just shatters my heart so much to see what you have been through and to watch you struggle to fight every day and night. You had, and still have, all those who have passed on watching over you. We will always have your back and so will spirit. All I have to do is call on them and they're beside you, protecting you all the time. They will never leave your side. You're my first born miracle girl. You have a long life ahead of you, it's going to be tough for you as you experience a thousand

and one different emotions but each time that happens we will be there to catch you. Every time I speak to you on the phone it's just wonderful to be able to hear you, and seeing how well you're doing is more than a miracle. I just can't find a word that's higher than that. When you told me you had five spirits around you, I knew straight away who they were, and every day you tell me the same thing, and that is your spirit family and your human family.

Every day she gets better and better. She forced herself to stand up but could only stand for a short period of time. The emotions are now running high; she smiles, laughs, and then she's angry at the whole world. Many, many millions of tears. She cries, I cry. She laughs, I laugh. It's so hard to keep my daughter in good spirits when we all know how much pain she's in and the heartache she suffered. So this is why people should love their family, talk to their family, help their family because you only have one family, one chance. Because, in a blink of an eye it can all turn into absolute heartache or even worse, die. You see it happen every day to other people but when it's someone in your family it's a whole new ball game. It doesn't just turn that person's life upside down but it destroys the whole family.

When I was about seven years old, I had a massive fetish for toy cars, if Mum gave me a doll I'd set it on fire with the other six dolls I had. So, I told Mum I was out of my lunch money for school, then I'd stop into the shop a buy myself a Matchbox car for 25 cents. Back then, I collected hundreds of them, I never knew what happened to them. As I got older Mum must have thrown them out when we were moving. I'd sit on the shed under a big peach tree playing with my cars until dark. Mum always came out looking for me when it had just gone dark. I heard these little footsteps walking towards me and I just sat there. I couldn't see nothing, so I kept playing with my cars. A boys voice said, "Hello." Well I can tell you now, it didn't take long to get off that roof. I told Mum about it but she just said that I had been out in the sun for too long, so I had dinner, a bath and went to bed. I was so tired that night and fell asleep straight away. The next morning I took my cars back up on the roof with a blanket and my breakfast. An hour into sorting my cars out, one flew off the roof so fast that it landed a couple of metres from the house. There was no wind and it was a boiling hot day because it was the middle of summer. Me, being seven at the time, never thought it could be something paranormal, so I just went on about my day and did what I loved, playing with cars on the roof. Later on in the afternoon at about 5-ish the boy spoke to me again. This time he was very loud and clear. He told me he used to live across the road from our house but he died. I asked him how, and he told me he was five years old when the accident happened. He was having a bath at 5 o'clock when he stood up to get the towel and slipped, hit his head, and drowned in the bathtub. I was scared but I got used to him. The next day Mum baked a cake and took it over to the neighbour. Mum started a conversation with the lady. She was lovely and in her late 60s. She thought I was a boy at first because I was always in jeans, a shirt, and a cap. She then told Mum how she had a son called Robby, and that he died a long time ago, he drowned in the bathtub. I was shocked to hear what she had told us, so I ran home and wouldn't play on the roof anymore.

We were there for a couple of years and packed up to go live out at Nobby, a little country town outside of Clifton. But, before we left he made himself known to the rest of my family by misbehaving in the house, and moving things around. Me and my sister, Shirley, were laying on Mum's bed doing our homework. It was about 7.30 pm and Mum's floor was pretty old, as was the house. There was a hole in the middle of the floor the size of a round cake tin. We left it alone but, anyhow, I finished my work before my sister and stood up to walk to my room when we heard a knocking sound coming from under the house. Oh my gosh it was scary, so I said out loud, "If anyone is there, move the tin," well, it didn't just move, it was as if someone had punched it really hard. So hard that it was level with my shoulder. That was it. We both bolted into the kitchen and told Mum. Mum went outside and looked under the house with a torch and there was nothing there, and no one could fit under the house because it was too low. We moved out and never heard from Robby again so I cant explain the tin flying up off the floor. Maybe it was Robby, I'd say he was angry because we were moving. From there, we moved to Nobby. Lots and lots of stuff happened there, I think I mentioned that at the start of my journey. But that little town was lovely, we didn't have to walk far to school, straight across the train tracks and we were at school. I remember walking home in the afternoon, the old station hasn't been used in years, so I called into the toilet. After I came out to wash my hands I saw this nurse standing in front of me for a split second. She was chubby and dressed in white. I was frozen, couldn't move and then she vanished. I ran home and told Mum but, as usual, Mum didn't believe me. So, every day I called in to the old station and sat there hoping to see her again. She never came back.

So, I decided to play in this little memorial park, a couple of seconds from our house. There was a sign and a photo on this steel post. The little memorial park I played in was in memory of a nurse called Sister Kenny, the same lady I saw at the railway station. I stopped telling my family about the things I saw because no one believed me anyway, so I stayed silent for most of my teenage years and into adulthood. As my gift got stronger I felt like spirit wasn't going to leave me alone. They certainly were pushing me in the right direction of the path I was meant to take.

Again, in my adult years the gift was pretty full on by then, but I kept silent about it pretty much all my life because I was pretty offended by people not believing me. It was very frustrating to say the least, so, again, I kept silent, until I told some of my family members, who had a giggle about it and about not believing me. Again I went silent about the whole thing. I just didn't care anymore about the gift. A negative impact towards me about my gift pretty much shut me down for years. I couldn't understand why no one believed me, I would never lie about something so serious. But today I have accepted who I am and I love what I do, I wouldn't change it for anything in the world. As long as I'm on this planet for, it's worth more to me than money because when you're gifted you were given this gift for a reason. For years I always asked myself, "Why am I here? What is my purpose in this world?" And now I know. It took many years of spirit trying to tell me but I have accepted it now and I think once you accept it then spirit teach you step by step. They have certainly guided me throughout my life and are still, and always are, going to be with me until it's my turn to cross over.

When I was 15 and still living at home, we had some paranormal activity going on in the house. Mum was pretty strict with us when it came to bed time. 8.30 pm on the dot. We were laying in bed, my sisters and I, as we had to share a room. Heavy footsteps walking down the hallway, I sang out, "Who's there?" The footsteps stopped right beside our bedroom door, I jumped out of bed and opened the door as fast as I could. There was nothing there, but the front door was wide open. Mum had said it was closed. I went to shut and lock the front door and looked up the very long driveway to the main road, and I could see this black figure gliding up the driveway and vanish. And, again, only one of my sisters and myself heard the footsteps. I was the only one to see the dark figure as my sister was too scared to come out with me.

Every night in this old farm house there was something different going on. My brother had a small pool table in his room. At midnight, we could hear the pool balls going down in the pockets. My brother couldn't get out of the room fast enough, and my sister Jo saw a ghostly figure flying over the top of the wardrobe. Doors would fly open in the middle of the night for no reason, and in the middle of summer too, so no wind would have caused that to happen. We decided to go for a walk one night. Big mistake. My other three sisters, my brother, and I went for a stroll at about 7.30 pm that night to visit an old neighbour who lived across the road from us. The same as our house, she too had a long, long driveway. It was pitch black so luckily it was a full moon that night so we could see a little bit of where we were walking to. It felt like it was taking forever to get there. Of course, I'm always the first one to hear anything. It was the heavy footsteps that we heard in the house, walking behind us but keeping its distance. I was so scared, so we started walking faster and every time we did it did, we started to test it out. We started to walk and stop, and so did it. We started running and so did it. We did that several times until my little sister was so scared that she started running fast, so we all took off too but the footsteps were left behind. We got to our neighbour's house in tears so she rang Mum up to come and pick us up.

Before dad passed, he had a job in a shipping yard and had to wear heavy steel-cap boots, so I'm guessing it was my father all along. He found us at the house we moved to after my uncle wouldn't tell him and he was behind us making sure we got to our neighbour's house in the dark. But, in saying that, he scared the life out of us to the point where we didn't do it again. If Dad had been alive and we did that we would have got a good old fashioned spanking. And we learnt our lesson, so when we wanted to visit the old lady, our neighbour, it was during the day.

I lived on the farm until I was sixteen, and I moved as I became pregnant with my first baby, Bronwen. I moved into my partner's house with their family but, eventually, they all moved to Brisbane. My partner and I were the only ones left. I raised my daughter by myself while her father was out every night, living the dream, while I stayed home looking after my newborn. This continued on for fifteen years, it was a very bad, violent relationship, but I didn't want to go back home. I had to learn to stand on my own two feet and cop what came at me. I was at breaking point in the end, so when my second daughter came along things got pretty bad. It was then I decided to pack up what I could and found a unit through the Salvos. I was so grateful for everything they did for me. I had to get my kids out of that house and away from their father. It was no life for them and myself, so starting all over on my own with two young children was absolutely scary as hell, but I knew I had to go for their sake and mine. I can't go into great detail as it is a very private and hard experience I endured. After I left, things got a bit easier for us but I was able to provide for the kids what I couldn't do before in my relationship. I have chosen to stay on my own for as long as I can. I don't need anyone in my life, only my family. My relationships showed me that I could survive on my own, so, to all you ladies out there who are in a situation with a violent person, be strong and walk away. There is a new life out there and no one should tell you how to live your own life. It's your life. I have one good female friend and my family and my spirit guides. What more could I want? My life is complete and karma is very, very real. Live your life now. Not tomorrow. Not next week. Live it now because we have numbers, and when our number is up that's it, we return to the spirit world.

I know it's very hard when you lose someone you love but because of my knowledge of the things I've learnt in my sixty years of life, I can honestly say we do live on. Remember they lived, they loved and laughed. When you're sad remember the good times you had with them, keep their memory alive because, believe me, they can hear and see you 24/7. They are not gone, don't ever say goodbye, just say see you later. Talk to them all the time because they love it. I live with spirit all the time and they are happy, they don't have to suffer in pain, they don't have to worry about anything. They are free from this painful world we live in.

So many mediums are gifted in many ways. We are all different, some can come up with a full name of a spirit, some only a letter, but, with me, I can see them, hear them, feel them, and talk to them. Sometimes they call me by my name, sometimes they just like to sit around me and have a good old chat. But when it's in the middle of the night, I have to be firm with them and make them go away. But in the spirit world there has to be the utmost respect for them. I always thank them for their help, that is a big must in the spirit world, if you don't show respect you get no messages. Nothing. Yes, they get angry, yes, sometimes they even swear, like my dad's spirit. Before Dad died he did not like bad words coming from kids' mouths. He would get so angry, even in spirit, I swore at him to save Bronwen, he didn't like that one bit. But always say sorry because they do forgive you. Coming from what I thought I was—just a plain, common person—to being a medium has totally turned my life around. And how to talk to spirit and how not to talk to spirit.

There are so many people suffering from heavy grief, spirit have trouble getting the message across. Please accept their death and you will see a big difference. I can't stress this enough: there is life after life. We will see our loved ones when we cross over, that I can promise you.

My thoughts about heaven, well, I haven't been there yet so I don't know. I believe we go to a different realm/dimension. But, what I do know is that they will be there when it's our time, to take us home. When my mum was in the nursing home and close to going she was looking over my shoulder, smiling. I asked her who was she looking at and she said her dad has come to take her home. I wasn't shocked because I knew it was her time. Mum passed over the next day, she was at peace. She just looked like a beautiful angel sleeping. On the day of the funeral I saw her standing near my little sister smiling at me, she loved us girls for doing a good job on her funeral. Mum and everybody else that I've loved and has passed over are 100% around me all the time, I know that for a fact because I hear them and see them. Dad is always zooming past my van, sometimes slow, sometimes very fast, so he must be in a hurry like he always was. I know he's going to be beside my daughter until she has fully recovered. Some of the things that she told me made my hair stand on end. She was being watched over for sure, she told me about this swishing sound and heard five spirits talking to her to go back and that it's not her time yet. Billions of people near death have experienced this. The supernatural, spirit world is so amazing, I just can't find the right word for it, the amazing part is when they show themselves to me, it's wonderful, just wonderful. I still don't like their little tricks they play on me though. But, all in all, I love every one of them. And animals are super cool and show themselves in many ways, you just have to look and listen. I meditate all the time now, I didn't think it would help but oh my gosh was I wrong. The things I've seen and heard after I meditate are mind blowing. My journey continues and every day there's something different.

The afterlife for children

The children's realm is a utopia that functions as a self-sustaining community, designed to provide its youthful inhabitants with all the amenities necessary for their comfort, education, pleasure, and joy. This heavenly domain was fashioned by inspired individuals who were guided by the greatest mind and it also serves as a sanctuary for those who pass away at a young age, where they can continue to learn and grow spiritually. Shedding any unnecessary knowledge, they gain spiritual insights that are essential to their progress. In this realm, all children have equal opportunities and spiritual rights regardless of age, just as in our mortal world.

Our ultimate goal is to attain perfect and eternal happiness. The death of a child at any age is the most painful experience life can bring. The grief it carries is a process to be managed, but it isn't something you ever really get over. The afterlife evidence has a lot to tell us about how our children are enjoying their lives in the afterlife. From the perspective of the child, early death leads to a beautiful childhood full of love and joy. All children go to heaven. Those who are, in spirit, given the special duty of managing childhood transitions already deeply know and love each child. Kind, loving, compassionate people in the afterlife take special care to make certain that children who are leaving their bodies will never know fear. If a beloved relative has transitioned before the child, then Grandma or Aunty Jane will come to the child's bedside and playfully lure the child away. Or otherwise, the deathbed greeter might be an angel. If a pet has gone ahead, then that pet might be there, too. The point is to make the moment of freedom from the body a happy time for the child, and to urge the child to leave the deathbed scene and the mourners as quickly and as playfully as possible.

Do children in heaven miss their families? Children in the afterlife very quickly adjust to their new lives. They have the ability to look in on us, and there is so much to do there in an atmosphere of perfect love where happiness is everyone's natural set point. They miss doing the things their family did, but know the family is okay and that soon they will all have a reunion.

Afterlife communication, with children

Many of those who have gone before us will attempt to send us signs of their survival, and this is especially true of our children of any age. Deep grief is a negative energy that can act as a barrier to communication, so as difficult as it may be for parents, it is important that we do what we can to manage our grief so it won't block contacts from our children who have gone before us. It is important that parents be alert for signs, even if there is a lot of doubt. Just think of them or get a picture of them, study their face and ask questions. They can hear you and they will respond to you. Sometimes signs can be numbers on coins; check the date of the coin if you come across one. It could mean something to you. Whether their favorite colour or song, there's just so many signs to look out for. I was just sitting here in my van like five minutes ago, and this little girl about three or four years of age often walks past in her pink pyjamas. I'm yet to find out who she is but she doesn't want to leave. I know she loves playing with my little grandson, Noah, so I'm guessing she's found a friend for life.

www.ingramcontent.com/pod-product-compliance
Lightning Source LLC
Chambersburg PA
CBHW041152110526
44590CB00027B/4209